Blurry Things

poems by

Nancee Annette Pace Cline

Finishing Line Press
Georgetown, Kentucky

Blurry Things

for Stephen

ACKNOWLEDGMENTS

Sincere appreciation to the following publications:

Amethyst Review: "To Court the Flash"
Central Texas Writers Society: the full version of "The Mood of In-between"
The Ekphrastic Review: "Booklover in a Mango Dress"
Flora Fiction: "The Black Witch Moth" and "Graceful, Gorgeous, Focused,
Wild"
Inscribe: "The Marshmallow Incident"
Shanti Arts: "Changing with the Seasons" and "I Like Blurry Things"
Starborne: The Journal of Autocosmology: "Little Girls Ponder Beauty
Unspeakable"

Special thanks to *Kate's Poetry Circle* who has listened to and encouraged me,
poem by poem.

Ongoing gratitude for poets Nicholas Samaras and Kathleen Dale for sharing
their gifts so generously.

And to Stephen, my Renaissance husband, a never-ending source of wisdom,
humor, and hugs.

Publisher: Leah Huete de Maines
Editor: Christen Kincaid
Cover Art: Grisham/Pace family photos
Author Photo: Stephen Cline
Cover Design: Elizabeth Maines McCleavy

Order online: www.finishinglinepress.com
        also available on amazon.com

Author inquiries and mail orders:
Finishing Line Press
PO Box 1626
Georgetown, Kentucky 40324
USA

Contents

Little Girls Ponder Beauty Unspeakable

The child Saint Teresa of Avila
twirled to the word *forever*
around, around, around.

For me, it was *infinity*,
a word that revealed itself
at the funeral of a great-grandmother.

My mother took me outside—a sobbing little girl.
She mistakenly believed
I was crying for the dead.

All the Last Mornings

My grandson does not say the word yesterday
but understands there is a past, a time behind him.

Instead of yesterday, he says "*last morning,*"
his sing-song voice finch-high.

Tuesday, his mother drove north with him
toward Mauna Kea, dawn just breaking.

Later, he explained to us, "*last morning*
the Sun was throwing *pink* at Hawaii!*"

All the last mornings—a meandering
river of clouds—wisping away.

A new child in an old world,
the Last Morning and the
First.

Breakfast on the Morning Lanai

In the first mouthful, a field of yellow suns—
a tree inside an almond, a kingdom inside a seed.

The first taste greets me from the cinnamon trees of Sri Lanka
and the blonde grain fields of Canada.

Banana, from its wild corner of my own backyard,
with coconut, and the prehistoric mango,

all three, renewing over and over, heavy, eternal sweetness.
And more seeds of chia, sesame, pumpkin,

each with a tiny blueprint for life.
Textures, tastes and nutrients from all directions, histories,

and sciences. Not one exists for my sake!
Each grows and flowers and fruits for its own bright glory.

With each spoonful, I welcome emissaries
from the growing greening blessed Earth

into my mouth. Morning communion.

Booklover in a Mango Dress
—after Winslow Homer's The New Novel, 1877

Shy in life, she is intrepid as a reader. She is not troubled
by foreign words or difficult themes, time travel

or conflicting passions. A seeker of solitude
far from the madding crowd, a new expression

she has adopted after reading a book from England.
She is wearing sunlight in her hair and a face full of serenity.

Perhaps the book is *Gone with the Wind,*
or a *Tale of Two Cities.* She might be chasing

a white rabbit through Wonderland,
or rafting down the Mississippi River.

Wherever in the world of literature she is, she is content.
Sometimes a stunning sentence will stop her;

she must live with it a while before she can read on.
She collects quotations, keeps them in a Chinese

lacquered jewelry box: random slips of paper, divine
or witty quotations about books, readers, authors.

She has enough bookmarks to count as a collection,
her favorites: a bright woven strip of cloth from Turkey,

and a fragrant one of sandalwood.
Her memory is an encyclopedia of characters,

their generosity and their flaws, recklessness
and fidelity, the tides and swirls of fate.

Does Winslow portray this pale bookworm in muted
colors? On the contrary! Her hair is a red-gold halo,

and the color of her dress, delicious.
Let's consider a new title for this painting:

Bookworm in Tangerine Marmalade
Future Poet Dressed in Papaya
Blue-stocking in Marigold

Besides the gorgeous color, there are details
on her dress easily overlooked, a black collar

and cuffs, and all those black buttons.
If this were a mystery they would matter,

details that would lead us to the bird named
Baltimore Oriole—orange and black, precise and tidy.

But there is no mystery here, except to the people who believe
that 'reading for pleasure' is a contradiction in terms.

She has memorized *The Lady of Shallot*
in a kind of ecstasy, but recited it to no one,

at least not yet. She does not want a Lancelot,
a Heathcliff, or a young Prince Hal.

If she falls in love in waking life, it will be
with a boy who also loves books,

and she will read aloud to him in green meadows,
and in the shade of lemon-scented eucalyptus trees.

He too will enjoy the clean green fragrance
of summer grass and Sweet Alyssum.

They will pause to enjoy the interruptions
of ladybugs and the song of meadowlarks.

They will read books aloud together every day,
even when they are old,

cultivating a sensitivity to enchantment,
and the habit of surrender.

In the Dream We Are Young Again

Two young mothers, long hair and bare feet,
sit together outside in the California sunshine,

shaded by a white wooden trellis,
quiet, at peace, breastfeeding butterflies,

a gently revolving circle
fluttering above and around them—

blue butterflies from Peru,
the ones that are purple

when seen from a different angle.

Smiling at Me

Our theme song is *Blue Skies*. On play dates,
we check the weather first as we turn

onto Alii Drive, both blue sea
and blue sky dominating our vision.

Some days, we sing *Gray Clouds smiling
at me, nothing but gray clouds, do I see.*

Sometimes, white clouds like whipped cream
in a blue bowl. Sometimes, he sings *pink*

and yellow and orange skies, too! I want
my grandson, three, to check-in with the sky,

clouds, and colors each day, a child
of the Milky Way, so he will know

his home. I ask Siri to play *Blue Skies,*
and expect the gravelly, laid-back

voice of Willie Nelson. But Siri
chooses Ella Fitzgerald, First Lady

of Soul, Queen of Jazz; her big sassy
voice fills the car. She does things with her

three-octave range he has never heard
before. She sings *scat*, imitating

an instrument with wordless syllables.
I watch my grandson in the rear-view

mirror, listening intently, eyes
big; the music receptors in his brain

leaping into new territory.
On the way home, he demands *More music!*

I ask Siri for *Somewhere over
the Rainbow*, and I expect to hear

the opening chords of Israel
Kamakawiwoʻoleʻs ukulele.

But Siri gives us Judy Garland:
sweet, round notes filled with longing, perfect

pitch and a beautiful, enduring question.
Rainbows, he sings, *Smiling at me.*

I Like Blurry Things

Especially clouds, how they float
and wisp, tower,
collapse.

I like the blur of emotions—
tears when joyful, laughter in grief,

the soft ambiguous border between
sleeping and waking,
the dreams of good sleepers.

I like reading between the lines,
and fluid interpretations,
wondering, guessing, secrets,

fictional characters who become lifelong friends,
soft-spoken mentors and shy children,

how sweet and tart overlap in cherries,
sweet and bitter in dark chocolate.

I like Impressionist art, sunlit pastels that drift,
poplars reflecting through wet shadows.

Oh! and the blending of families in naming:
        dragonfly
        maidenhair fern
        baby's breath
        tiger shark
        buttermilk sky.

The Marshmallow Incident

She twirls in the waiting line,
as only a 7-year-old can,

a marshmallow package over
her head, a celebration

of sugar and campfire lore,
the check-out lady so charmed

she can hardly do her work.
"Twenty percent more!" my grand-

daughter reads the label with glee!
"Twenty percent more WHAT?

More Fun? More Sugar?
Money? Marshmallows?"

She is twirling again, giddy
with the possibilities.

The checker brushes away
joy-tears, she cannot answer,

nor does she know.
My Charlotte waltzes away,

a blur of pink and vanilla,
the marshmallows held firmly

against her heart.

The Birds of Eden

The Garden, the wild and perfect habitat,

as yet un-named, un-tamed, un-violated,
a mutually enhancing bio region,

I am not an Adam. I am not
an Eve. I am not snake.

I am warbler-of-the-dawn.
My song, a celebration; my flight,

joy; my nest, a creative endeavor
of great satisfaction.

I am messenger from the Great-Ever-Loving One.
We bookend the days;

I sing for the mornings, my sisters
sing for the night. We sing!

It is our privilege, our glory.
The green world our playground,

places for hiding and seeking, in sun green
and shadow green, a thousand

greens, and blues—a celestial poem.
The Earth is our nest, but the Universe our home.

The Adam and the Eve are here, newcomers,
children just learning the language and nuance

of life. A thousand-fold live here,
 and for eons, we have maintained

the Great Harmony.
We are the play, the gift,

the high notes
of the Great-Ever-Loving Song.

To Court the Flash

A damaged oak, deep-rooted, stands
in a lonely place.

See the deep scar that spirals down the trunk?
The path of lightning.

Imagine wave after wave of heat,
the white light scorching,

the thunder-boom blasting the earth.
With your eyes closed, touch the scar,

a mingle of rough and smooth,
the path both living art and proof

of the god's visit:
a moment of encounter beyond time,

a quicksilver knowing,
then the return to real time, tree time,

left with much to heal,
much to contemplate.

Did I speak of silver? The strike, pure white,
but the after-glow silver.

The following spring,
a hint of silver shimmers in new leaves.

Legend says oaks are favored by the sky god.
Legend says the most beloved trees

are struck again and again.
These chosen trees continue

to court the flash.

The Leaves Are Full of Children

Always and everywhere, the leaves are full of children,
the hidden laughter in the foliage, eternal.

Now, here, one little boy in an orange tree,
twigs caught in the silk of his hair,

rough bark scraping bare legs,
climbing branch by branch,

testing gravity, testing balance,
yielding to the Sirens' call "higher, higher!"

He reaches for a golden globe,
but his hand is too small,

the orange tumbles to the soft shade underneath,
rolls toward yellow sunshine.

Please notice the perfect symmetry of the wrist,
the ankle, the collarbone,

the delicate hinge of the eyelid,
the flutter of dark lashes,

and always, movement, fluid as breath,
the rise and fall, the challenge

directly in front of him,
insistent, beguiling.

From crawl to walk to gallop,
from cooing to questioning,

curiosity: the engine of becoming.
As he begins singing, let us

acknowledge the miracle of the voice box,
saliva on the agile tongue,

the miniscule anvil and hammer of the ear,
the devotion of it all working together,

one universe orbiting the heart,
beating with light and electricity.

Praise every beautiful curve,
angle and plane of his young body.

His laughter spills out
like windchimes in the wind.

Graceful, Georgeous, Focused, Wild

1. *San Diego Mountains*

Once upon a winding road, I met
somebody new—a friend, a foe, a guide—

while driving the forest curves, the slow
twists of everyday afternoon light,

in and out of scented evergreen shade.
In those days I drove a Carmen Ghia,

low to the ground, sandy beige
with a root beer top that sparkled with sun.

That afternoon, driving home, windows open,
I sensed a presence next to me—

a mountain lion running gracefully
beside my shoulder, tawny beige fur,

black ear tips, wild, focused, fluid.
Immediately, my heart made itself known,

even the mountain lion could hear it.
I did two things simultaneously—

slowly rolled up the hand crank window,
and gently took my foot off the gas pedal.

For a few breath-holding moments,
we coasted in tandem.

2. *The South Bay of Los Angeles*

Decades later, soon after my parents
died, I dreamt of the mountain lion.

The scene, the patio of their home,
the yucca in pale flower,

June gloom, a typical morning sky.
I was sitting in their white patio chair,
gazing toward the eucalyptus.
This time, I saw his yellow-green eyes

and he held mine as he approached,
graceful, gorgeous, focused, wild.

My mountain lion placed his heavy, square head
on my shoulder. Cheek to cheek,

warm fur, warm breath, against my face.
And we stayed that way,

breathing in tandem.

She Sings a Lullaby Over Bread

Charlotte is wearing my handwoven, poinsettia-red apron
from Honduras. At ten, the apron finally fits her.

She is grating orange peel into bread dough, and singing:
What child is this, who laid to rest, on Mary's lap is sleeping?

I imagine Mary at fourteen—exhausted by her night
of childbirth, limp and languid, forehead damp,

pupils dilated—in the soft afterglow
of surrender and amazement.

My Charlotte, at ten, knows nothing of that,
but she has two dogs (one old, one young)

and understands the ox and the ass leaning in close,
all warmth and fur, breathing in and out together.

When angels greet with anthems sweet . . .
Raise, raise a song on high, the virgin sings a lullaby . . .

Charlotte, with shining eyes, and flour
on her forehead, an ordinary, beloved virgin,

sings a lullaby over bread
for Christmas morning.

Why We Save Them

First are the fragile ballerinas, periwinkle
and white, frozen in arabesque.

I return them carefully to a separate silver box.
Then the six swirly glass icicles of mostly blue.

The seashells and abalone are decorated with feathers,
from our cold morning walks across Morro Bay,
our very beginning.

> *We are symbol-making creatures.*

Then, the ones from the grandparents, storybook
illustrations: Jeremiah Puddle Duck, our favorite.

And here—a plush giraffe,
a running reindeer, a miniature cathedral.

Some were made by our children,
here –a naked baby Jesus, anatomically correct.

Some by artists—hand painting on blown glass—
a Hawaiian turtle swimming in turquoise.

> *We are meaning-making mammals.*

I gather a little pile of the ones Corrine made over the years:
tiny ice skates, clothespin sheep, lacey snowflakes.

And here, to celebrate your talent—
a golden harp, a lute, a trumpet.

Lots of gold and silver, and white for holy,
sparkles and glitter for starlight on snow.

> *We are dream makers.*

Here is a flock of angels,
some soft, some glass, some blond.

Here is a chocolate brown angel from Uganda.
Here's one with her gaze focused far, far away.

We, too, follow wonder.

The Giant Black Witch Moth

Opened like a Chinese lacquered fan
Darkened through dynasties and for night
Intricate design of ruffles and lace
Carries a message from spirit beyond

Darkened through dynasties and for night
Why leave the eaves of the morning lanai?
Carries a message from spirit beyond
Crossing by drift from the afterlife

Why leave the eaves of the morning lanai?
The spiders of April waiting below
Crossing by drift from the afterlife
A flick of the wrist the wing the web

The spiders of April waiting below
Opened like an antique Chinese fan
A flick of the wrist the wing the web
Darkened through dynasties and for night

Origami Dream for the Bereaved

A circle of mothers—yours, your grandmothers,
and your greats—surrounds you.

The living and the dead work together,
quiet and focused, folding

origami flowers from gold and silver foil,
speaking only when we finish one

—a day lily, lotus, rose bud—
holding each up for all to see,

and then acknowledging one attribute
or virtue of the newly lost son:

Thoughtful / Sincere / Funny.

Altogether, a shimmering bouquet.

Hello Covid

I stop to get eyedrops and Chapstick,
glance up into my bathroom mirror.
On my white face I see bright red lips.
I have been too ill to wear any make-up,
and I have never worn red lipstick,
ever (*redheads don't wear red*).

This momentarily interrupts packing
for my trip to the Emergency Room.
I lean in to see better,
try to rub off the red,
but it does not come off.
One tiny mystery—actually a *pretty* mystery.

Later, I discover on the web that blue lips
are an uncommon symptom of late, severe
Covid. It signals a lack of oxygen in the blood:
indicates *acute hypoxia respiratory failure*.
Sometimes, the article says, lips turn *cherry red*.

Even though my diagnosis is terrible, I remember
the moment of surprise. I was a little girl again,
allowed to wear my mother's lipstick
for a ballet recital.
Seeing my young innocent face
in the mirror—*Oh! Is that really me?*

*

It is like the scene in a movie
       the table is set glasses plates silverware flowers
       everyday miscellaneous and you think 'this is my life'
       but then the field surgeon or midwife with a mighty backhand
       sweeps everything crashing to the floor
       and corrects you looking at the bare table
       says "no *this* is your life"

The movie set morphs into the local Emergency Room and the bare table
is covered with scores of schematics
      diagramming the intricacies of your heart and blood
      the delicate never-ending work of your lungs
      the ongoing dedication of your spleen liver nerves skeleton
        digestive system
      all systems working together unbelievably complicated

I am an innocent bystander as two armies fight
for the tiny patch of land that is me

You don't recognize this part of your life
appreciate it   love it   but your autonomic system
is most of who you are
      the pretty broken glass
on the floor
is just the very outside edge

I hear the high sparkling notes of glass
      shattering
see that mighty backhand
          again   and again
sweeping everything else
      aside

Dreaming for Soldiers

I went to a place of wounded soldiers. Thousands of them on cots
close together, lined up far into the distance. More than my eyes
could see, more than my lips could count.

I had been given three jobs to do there:

First, give each soldier a small teacup of cream—rich, heavy, sweet,
in the same dainty flowered teacup.

Second, listen to their stories if they wanted to talk. Most
were silent, but some told of battles. One spoke of the beach at
Normandy. I listened, but didn't respond.

My third job: kiss each soldier good night. I kissed them on their
foreheads like children. Except the ones who were dying; I kissed
them on the lips.

The Lure

A monkey, seated on a golden music box,
wears a scarlet Persian vest.

Underneath the box a key turns,
and 96 steel teeth pluck on a brass cylinder,

playing *Phantom of the Opera*, while
the monkey gently clangs the cymbals.

My grandson is terrified of this, and yet
the terror lures him back to our library where

it waits for him, silently, on the bookshelf.
My grandson doesn't know

the story of the monster behind the mask,
the panic in the Paris opera house,

the terrible twisted choices,
the love story gone berserk.

He only knows the little brown monkey
is dangerous, gazing upwards as if waiting

for disaster, as if watching
for the great chandelier to fall.

The lure for my granddaughter is
the dark Angel of Music, the singing

beyond the music box, the emotional range,
the vocal range, the pathos.

As a little girl, she sang all the time—
to her Mickey and Minnie Mouse dolls,

on our long walk through Angkor Watt
in stifling heat.

Now she sings in the shower at full volume,
and while making Sunday pancakes,

and when descending a circular staircase
in Vienna, testing the echoes.

At 14, with long legs and soft eyes,
she becomes *Christine*,

descending the cold stone stairs
to the dark underworld

below.

The Mood of In-between

Looking at the camera, not smiling, but not stiff either,
the three are leaning against a car, the girl in the middle
with her father on one side, her brother on the other.

Their feet are blurred though, as if they are not connected
to the earth, rather hovering above. They are holding
onto each other to keep from floating away.

The girl is the focus, the heart, the centerpiece of both
the photograph and this poem. She has one of those old-fashioned
sad names, and mousy brown hair in a whole extended family

—backwards and sideways—of mousey-browns.
She is a tenth-grade girl in East Texas, on the edge of a world war.
Her dress is a hand-me-down from her distant sisters,

she doesn't have anything of her own, but she does have
an admirable English teacher who offers her book after book
of literature good for the soul.

You know how the fifth child resents the birth of the sixth?
Giving up the sweet spot as the darling of the family,
to a new and demanding crier? The girl allows

her younger brother to hang on to her arm for the photograph,
but that's about all. He is dressed-up like Charles Lindberg
in an aviator jacket, cap and goggles. He is too young

to be without a mother, and is quite lost, but can
pretend to be *Lucky Lindy* whenever he needs to,
fly the big beautiful sky of his imagination.

This sky is empty though, the season too late
for morning glories, too early for plum blossoms.
The date for this photograph? Perhaps it is November of 1941,

in the brief corridor of time between the mother's death
and the bombing of Pearl Harbor.
Hardly enough time to get one's balance.

These two kids don't know why their mother died,
and somehow know they are not allowed to ask.
In the silence they feel as empty and pointless as tumbleweeds.

The vines growing up over the porch, gray in the photo,
are only leaves left behind after the morning glory petals
have blown away, and outside of the photo to the left

is a porch swing where the girl sat *just last year* and read
Julius Caesar aloud with her parents. Reading Shakespeare
was like seeing the ocean for the first time! Which she never has.

The man—the father, the widower—is wearing a suit,
so something special is happening—maybe a social gathering,
and his musical instrument is already in the car,

a *watermelon bowl back* mandolin. You can't see it,
but underneath his hat, there is a bluegrass tune running around.

The girl is small for her age, and she started her period late,
only after her mother died, and—*like a million uninformed girls*—
believes that she is dying,

and no one to tell or ask for help except her grieving father
and an irrelevant small brother. She hides her fear, her blood,
her embarrassment. Faded dress, private face, indifferent sky,

there is really no hint that her heart is a Crayola box of colors!
The arts will be her lasting love: every form from Renaissance
painting, to musical theater, to sculpture. She will nurture

this love in the lonely times. Of which there are many.
She will survive. She will be the first female in her family to go
to college. To the astonishment of her extended mousy browns,

she will give birth to three red-headed children.
She will see the deep blue Pacific Ocean,
which is a lot like reading Shakespeare for the first time.

Far into the future she will complain to her doctors that she
doesn't feel quite right, that her feet don't touch the ground.
The doctors stare past her. How could they possibly

understand unless they could see the proof in this old photograph?
These three, the girl in the middle, hovering above the earth,
caught in all the in-betweens.

Changing with the Seasons

For the springtime of my life, I was a letter,

>   the sensitive greeting handwritten on pastel paper,
>   the airmail post to a distant pen pal,
>   a declaration of love for my mother, illustrated in crayon.

In the summer, I grew into an essay,

>   the college thesis typed on onion skin paper,
>   book reviews, creative non-fiction.

Now, in autumn, I am haiku.

>   Instead of the long swim across the blue bay,
>   I am the entry into the water—
>   movement from vertical to horizontal.
>   A splash illuminated.

Will there be a time when *one perfect word* will suffice?

>   In hospital, with Death herself
>   meandering the hallway,
>   I re-imagined the dictionary,
>   searched the thesaurus of my memory,
>   narrowed myself down to only
>   one milky opalescent word:
>   *cherish.*

And my near-winter heart is satisfied.

End notes

"Little Girls Ponder Beauty Unspeakable"
 Teresa of Avila—a mystic and a saint, born in Spain, 1515

"Smiling at Me"
 Blue Skies, lyrics written by Irving Berlin
 Somewhere Over the Rainbow, lyrics by Yip Harburg

"The Leaves are Full of Children"
 a line from *Four Quartets*, by TS Eliot.
 Dedicated to three little boys: Aspen, Lucci and Valentino

"She Sings a Lullaby Over Bread for Christmas Morning"
 What Child is This? lyrics by William Chatterton Dix

"Why We Save Them"
 We are meaning making/ symbol making. . . from notes
 taken from documentary film *Journey of the Universe* by
 Brian Swimme

"The Lure"
 Phantom of the Opera musical by Andrew Lloyd Webber,
 novel by Gaston Leroux

Nancee Cline is a lifetime lover of the written word. She holds a master's degree in Interdisciplinary Humanities, as well as two certificates in Theological Education. She has tutored and taught every age group from Montessori pre-school through community college adults.

Nancee and her husband, Stephen, have always chosen to live in quiet and beautiful places: California redwoods, an intentional community on the Great Plains, the San Diego mountains, the beach in Carpinteria, and for the last 22 years, on the Big Island of Hawaii (the one with the active volcano) a place where their twin sons and two grandchildren are happy to visit.

When not reading, writing, or studying, she dances hula, bakes peasant bread, and gardens her half acre of wild green.

www.ingramcontent.com/pod-product-compliance
Lightning Source LLC
Chambersburg PA
CBHW020223090426
42734CB00008B/1201